An
ALICE
IN
BIBLELAND ®
Storybook

# The STORY Of CREATION

D0122532

Written by Alice Joyce Davidson
Illustrated by Victoria Marshall

Text copyright ©1984 by Alice Joyce Davidson
Art copyright ©1984 by The C.R. Gibson Company
Published by The C.R. Gibson Company
Norwalk, Connecticut 06856
Printed in the United States of America
All rights reserved
ISBN 0-8378-5066-5
D.L. TO: 201-1988

Alice was a little girl
Who went to Bible School.
She learned the Ten Commandments,
And she followed every rule.

She had a Bible storybook,
With Bible pictures, too,
And reading it was just about
Her favorite thing to do.

One day as she was reading
How God made everything,
An airmail bird brought Alice
This note beneath his wing:

"Reading is the magic key
To take you where you want to be."

Her book became a magic screen.
The screen grew tall and wide,
Then Alice took a little walk
To Bibleland inside.

Alice went far back in time
Before the world began
So she could see the wonders
Of God's creative plan.

There was nothing yet to stand on,
Nothing yet to see,
But Alice thought, "I'm not afraid
For God is near to me."

Then God began to make things.
He made heaven, earth, and light.
God called the bright light "day,"
And He called the darkness "night."

And God saw everything was good,
And everything was splendid,
And the evening and the morning
Of the very first day ended.

The second day Alice watched
God create the sky
Filled with lovely fluffy clouds
That slowly drifted by.

And God saw everything was good,
And everything was splendid,
And the evening and the morning
Of the second day had ended.

The third day of creation
More changes came to be.
God moved the waters of the earth
And made the land and sea.

Alice was quite happy
To stand on land once more.
While God created lots of plants
That were not there before.

Clover, grass, and buttercups
Grew beneath her feet.
Apple, pear, and fig trees
Gave Alice treats to eat.

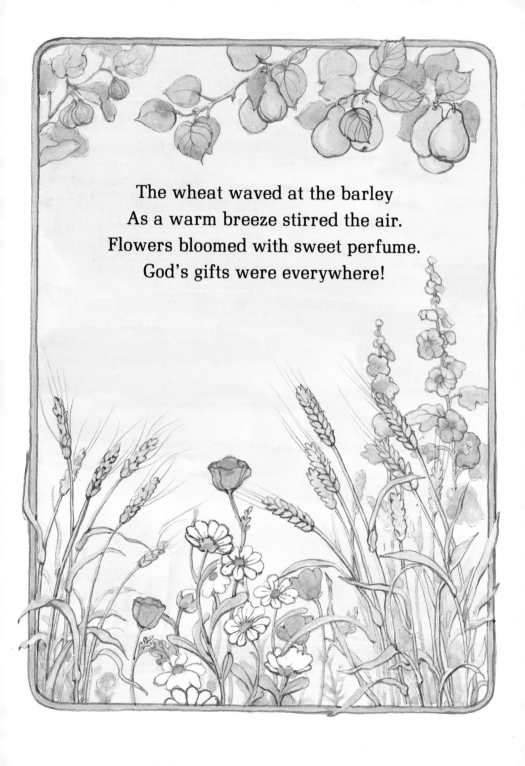

The wheat waved at the barley
As a warm breeze stirred the air.
Flowers bloomed with sweet perfume.
God's gifts were everywhere!

And God saw everything was good,
And everything was splendid,
And the evening and the morning
Of the third new day had ended.

The fourth day God made stars and lights.
The biggest was the sun.
The sun shone during daytime,
The moon, when day was done.

And God saw everything was good,
And everything was splendid,
And the evening and the morning
Of the fourth new day had ended.

Alice wished for company.
The fifth day brought her wish.
God filled the sky with birds that fly,
And in the seas placed fish.

And God saw everything was good,
And everything was splendid,
And the evening and the morning
Of the fifth new day had ended.

The sixth day God created
Beasts both great and small,
And as He did a "thank You"
Was heard from one and all.

The elephants all trumpeted,
The cattle all said moo.
Donkeys brayed, and lions roared,
The horses whinnied, too.

Hyenas laughed, the sheep said baa,
A lion roared again.
A puppy barked, a kitten meowed,
And Alice said, "AMEN!"

Then God continued working
On His creative plan.
With love, and in His image,
God created MAN.

God created MAN and WOMAN,
A husband and a wife.
He put them both in charge of all
The things He brought to life.

God told them to have babies,
And to take the best of care
Of all of His creations
On land, and sea, and air.

And God saw everything was good,
And everything was splendid,
And the evening and the morning
Of the sixth new day had ended.

On the seventh day God rested
From the work which He had done.
God made that day a Sabbath day,
A very holy one.

Alice walked back through the screen,
Which became her book once more,
And knew more how the world began
Than she had known before.

And when she went to Bible School,
She sang this song of praise
About how God made everything
In only seven days.

Glory! Glory! Glory!
Glory to our King,
For out of nothing He has made
Every living thing!

Glory! Glory! Glory!
A song of praise is due
To God who made the whole wide world
Including Me and You!